NnOoPp
QqRr
SsTtUu
VvWw
XxYyZz

volume **3**

BIG BIRD'S SESAME STREET DICTIONARY

FEATURING JIM HENSON'S SESAME STREET MUPPETS

LETTERS E–G

by Linda Hayward

illustrated by Joe Mathieu

Editor in Chief: Sharon Lerner

Art Directors: Grace Clarke and Cathy Goldsmith
with special thanks to Judith M. Leary

Funk & Wagnalls, Inc./Children's Television Workshop

Ee

A B C D **E** F G H I J K L M N O P Q R S T U V W X Y Z

each   Each means every or every one.

Each of us has a balloon. **Each** balloon is a different color.

ear   Your ear is the part of your body that you use for hearing. Look up the word body.

tic toc

Bert is holding the clock next to his **ear.** He can hear the clock ticking.

early   Early means too soon.

HOOPER'S STORE

PARADE TODAY

Bert, did I miss the parade?

No, Ernie, you're **early.** It hasn't started yet.

early   Early can also mean near the beginning.

The sun rises **early** in the morning.

earth Earth is the name of the planet on which we live.

Astronaut Grover can see the planet **earth.**

earth Earth is also another word for ground.

The **earth** in Farmer Grover's garden is good for growing carrots.

easy When something is easy, you do not have to work hard to do it.

eat When you eat, you swallow food.

egg An egg is a round or oval thing that holds a baby animal until it is ready to be born.

The baby robin is being born. It is hatching from its **egg.**

eight Eight is a number. Eight is one more than seven.

Oscar has **eight** tin cans in his used-can collection.

eighteen   Eighteen is a number. Eighteen is ten plus eight more.

Ernie has ten red marbles and eight blue marbles. He has **eighteen** marbles all together.

either   Either means one or the other.

Oh, Oscar! You can have **either** the red roses or the stinkweed.

Red roses? Yuk! I'll take the stinkweed.

elbow   Your elbow is in the middle of your arm. Your arm bends at the elbow. Look up the word body.

Betty Lou has a bandage on her **elbow.**

elephant   An elephant is a big gray animal with a long nose called a trunk.

Which of these animals is an **elephant**?

elevator   An elevator takes people or things up and down in a building.

Grover the **elevator** operator operates an **elevator**.

eleven   Eleven is a number. Eleven is ten plus one more.

Bert has ten socks that match and one sock that does not match. He has **eleven** socks all together.

empty   When something is empty, there is nothing or no one in it.

The cookie jar is full.

The cookie jar is **empty**.

end   The end is the very last part of something.

Big Bird is standing at the **end** of the line.

end   When something ends, it is over.

The play will **end** when the curtain comes down.

THE END

The SESAME STREET PLAYERS

energy Energy is power to do work. People and machines need energy. Energy for your body comes from food. Energy for machines can come from burning fuel or from the sun.

Farmer Grover uses **energy** from the sun to heat his henhouse.

engine An engine is a machine that makes something go.

This tractor will not go unless I turn on the **engine**.

CHUG CHUG

engineer An engineer is someone who knows how to build machines or roads or bridges or buildings.

When I grow up, I am going to be an **engineer** and build real bridges.

engineer A train engineer is someone who drives a train.

Cookie the train **engineer** is driving the Cookie Express.

enjoy When you enjoy yourself, you have a good time.

I **enjoy** feeding pigeons.

Here, pigeons!

I **enjoy** counting pigeons. 1, 2, 3, 4, 5... five well-fed pigeons!

enough When you have enough, you have as much as you need.

There are six grouches and six garbage cans. There are **enough** garbage cans for everyone!

enter When you enter, you go in.

entrance The entrance is where you go in.

I, Grover, will **enter** through the **entrance**.

envelope An envelope is a paper container for a letter.

Big Bird has written a letter. He is putting it into an **envelope**.

equal When things are equal, they are the same in number or size.

I have three presents.

I have three presents.

The Busby twins have an **equal** number of presents.

equipment   Equipment is a set of things you need to do a job.

Biff and Sully are carrying **equipment** to repair the street.

erase   When you erase something, you wipe it away.

> Baby Breeze, **erase** that picture.

teacher

eraser   An eraser is something you use to erase with.

Bert has eight **erasers** in his **eraser** collection.

escalator   An escalator is a stairway with moving steps. Escalators can take you up or down.

DOWN

even   When two things or people are even, they are at the same level. They can also be at the same distance from a certain point.

Grover and Betty Lou are riding side by side on the **escalator.** They are **even** with each other.

even   Even also means smooth, flat, or level.

Farmer Grover is raking his garden so the ground will be **even.**

ever   Ever means at any time or at all times.

As our story ends, Marshal Grover is riding into the sunset. Will he **ever** return to Sesame Gulch? Will he **ever** capture Bad Bart? Will he **ever** sit on Fred the right way?

every   Every means each one or all.

Every morning the sun comes up in the east.

except   Except means leaving out.

Everybody **except** Big Bird is in Big Bird's nest.

Hey, everybody! What about me?

excited   You feel excited when you expect something wonderful.

I wonder what is in this package. Oh, I'm so **excited**! Maybe it's a bag of birdseed or a pillow for my nest or…

exercise   When you exercise, you make your muscles work.

Exercise is good for you.

Betty Lou and Farley like to **exercise**.

Exercise is good fun!

running

pushups

jumping

biking

dancing

somersaults

chin-ups

situps

leapfrog

toe touching

exit   The exit is the way out.

The Alphabeats are leaving through the **exit.**

expect   When you expect something, you think it will happen.

expensive   When something is expensive, it costs a lot of money.

explain   When you explain something, you try to help someone else understand it.

extra   When you have an extra amount of something, you have more than you need.

eye   Your eye is a part of your face. You use your eyes for seeing. Look up the word face.

Which picture does not belong?

In each big square there are three pictures of things that begin with the letter **E.** Can you find the picture that does not belong?

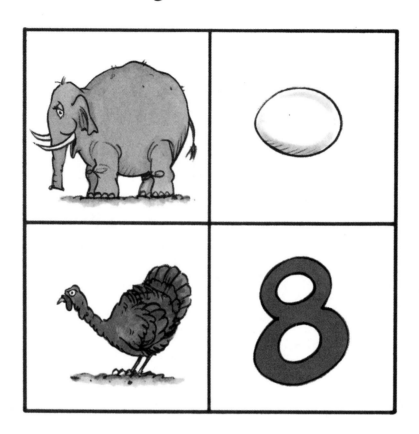

face   Your face is the front part of your head.

Can you name the parts of Bert's **face**?

eyebrow
eye
forehead
nose
cheek
ear
mouth
chin

fact   A fact is something that is true.

The tallest living animal is the giraffe.

Is that true?

It's a **fact**, Big Bird.

factory   A factory is a building where many people work together to make something.

Figgy Fizz Co. Inc.

BOTTLE CAPS

Figgy Fizz

Everyone at the Figgy Fizz **factory** has a different job.

fair   When you are fair, you try to treat everyone the same way.

That's not **fair**!

That's **fair**!

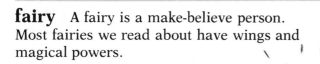

fairy A fairy is a make-believe person. Most fairies we read about have wings and magical powers.

There is a picture of a **fairy** in Big Bird's book of **fairy** tales.

> A **fairy** tale is a story about **fairies** or other make-believe creatures.

fall Fall is the name of a season. Fall comes after summer.

> In the **fall**, the leaves turn beautiful colors.

> **Fall** and autumn are two different names for the same season.

fall When something falls, it drops down.

> I love to watch the rain **fall** because I love to count the raindrops.

false When something is false, it is not true.

TRUE OR FALSE!

> Hi, everybody! I'm Guy Smiley, everybody's favorite game show host. And here is everybody's favorite game show— TRUE OR **FALSE**?

> Me called Big Bird. True or **false**?

> Hi! I'm Oscar the Grouch. True or **false**?

What is your answer?

family A family is a group of people who are related.

This is my **family.**

I'm her mother.

I'm her father.

I'm her sister.

I'm her brother.

famous When you are famous, many people know who you are.

Big Bird is a **famous** bird.

fan A fan makes a breeze that helps to keep you cool.

I am cooling off in front of an electric **fan.**

I am cooling off with a paper **fan.**

far When something is far, it is a long distance away.

The moon is very **far** from the earth.

Earth

Moon

farm A farm is a place where people grow food and raise animals.

farmer A farmer is someone who works on a farm.

Farmer Grover grows corn on his **farm.** He feeds the corn to his pigs.

fast When something moves fast, it moves very quickly.

The hare runs **fast.** The tortoise walks slowly.

fasten When you fasten something, you make it hold together.

Fasten your seat belt, Prairie Dawn.

fat When something is fat, it is big around.

Some pretzels are **fat.**

Some pretzels are thin.

father A father is a man who has a child.

This is my **father.** I call him Dad. My **father** is putting a bandage on my knee. Thanks, Dad.

favorite The one that is your favorite is the one you like the best.

My **favorite** food is birdseed.

My **favorite** food is cabbage.

BIRD SEED

fear When you fear something, you are afraid of it.

There is nothing to **fear.** The monsters on Sesame Street are friendly.

feather A feather is something that grows on a bird. Feathers help birds to stay warm. They also help them to fly.

Aha! I have found a **feather.** I wonder where it came from.

feed When you feed people or animals, you give them food.

POP CORN

Bert likes to **feed** the pigeons.

feel   When you feel something, you touch it. Different things feel different.

I like to **feel** a kitten's fur because it is soft.

A bug **feels** with the **feelers** on top of its head.

feel   Feel also means to be or seem a certain way.

LITTLE JERRY AND THE MONOTONES SING ABOUT THEIR FEELINGS

I **feel** happy.

I **feel** sad.

I **feel** hungry.

I **feel** mad.

fence   A fence is a kind of wall that is usually outdoors. A fence is usually built to keep things in or out.

I wonder why this **fence** is here.

Oh!

few   Few means a small number.

Bert has a **few** bottle caps in the red box. He has many bottle caps in the blue box.

field   A field is a large piece of ground where there are no buildings and usually no trees.

Farmer Grover is planting seeds in his **field.**

fifteen   Fifteen is a number. Fifteen is ten plus five more.

Cookie the baker made ten round cookies and five square cookies. He made **fifteen** cookies all together.

fight When you fight, you struggle against someone or something.

The job of the fire **fighters** is to **fight** fires.

find When you find something, you discover it. Sometimes you find things by accident. Sometimes you look for something until you find it.

Egad! I, Sherlock Hemlock, have **found** a mystery. Where is this water coming from?

I will have to keep searching until I **find** the answer.

finger Your finger is a part of your hand. Most people have five fingers on each hand and ten fingers all together. Look up the word body.

How does this monster count to fifteen?

On his **fingers**!

fill When you fill a container, you put something into it until it will hold no more.

Ernie will **fill** the bathtub with water. When it is **full**, he will take a bath.

finish When you finish, you come to the end.

Cookie the baker has **finished** baking a cake.

Soon he will **finish** eating the cake.

fire   Fire is flame, heat, and light caused by something burning.

fire engine   A fire engine is a truck that carries fire fighters and their equipment to a fire.

fire fighter   A fire fighter is someone whose job is to put out fires.

The **fire fighters** drove their **fire engine** to the **fire.**

first   When something is first, it comes before all the others.

Cookie Monster is **first** in line.

COOKIES

FREE COOKIE TO **FIRST** IN LINE!

fish   A fish is an animal that lives in the water. A fish breathes through special openings called gills. Most fish have fins and scales.

Bert is watching the **fish**. The **fish** are watching Bert.

fish   To fish means to try to catch a fish.

Herry Monster likes to **fish.**

fit   When something fits, it is the right size or shape.

five   Five is a number. Five is one more than four.

Herry Monster is eating **five** carrots for lunch.

fix   When you fix something, you make it right again.

Betty Lou will **fix** the broken faucet.

flag   A flag is a piece of cloth. Most flags have special colors and a special meaning. Every country has its own flag.

Grover is holding the American **flag.**

flat　When something is flat, it is not bumpy.

What do monsters eat that is square and green and **flat** as a pancake?

A square green pancake!

flavor　The flavor of something is its taste.

I love the **flavor** of chocolate ice cream.

I love the **flavor** of chocolate, too. Heh, heh. I love spinach with chocolate sauce.

float　When something floats, it stays on top of the water.

Herry's toy boat can **float** on water.

floor　The floor is the part of the room you walk on. Sometimes the floor is covered with a carpet.

What is the first thing a monster puts on when he gets out of bed in the morning?

He puts his feet on the **floor**!

flour　Flour is a powder that is made from grain. It is used to make cake, bread, and other things to eat.

Cookie the baker uses **flour** to make cookies.

flower　A flower is the part of the plant that has petals. Many flowers have sweet smells and pretty colors.

Three of these things do not belong here. A stinkweed is a kind of weed. It definitely belongs here. But a rose and a tulip and a daisy are all **flowers**. They don't belong here.

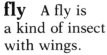

fly A fly is a kind of insect with wings.

Look!
There is another **fly**!
I love to count **flies.**
1, 2, 3, 4, 5…
five fabulous **flies**!
Wonderful!

fly When things fly, they move in the air.

Some birds **fly** and some don't.

Grover likes to **fly** his airplane.

Betty Lou likes to **fly** her kite.

fly When you fly something, you make it move in the air.

fold When you fold something, you bend one part of it over another part.

Bert likes to **fold** laundry.

food Food is what we eat. All living things need food to help them grow.

Bert is feeding the pigeons some pigeon **food.** Ernie is feeding the plants some plant **food.**

follow When you follow something, you move along behind it.

Cookie Monster will **follow** anyone with cookies.

foot A foot is an amount of distance. There are twelve inches in a foot. Look up the word inch.

Bert's paper-clip chain is one **foot** long.

foot Your foot is the part of your body at the end of your leg. Look up the word body.

forehead Your forehead is the part of your face above your eyebrows. Look up the word face.

There is a fly on the Count's **foot** and a fly on his **forehead**.

Let me count them. 1... 2... two flies!

forest A forest is a place where many trees grow.

Prairie Dawn is hiking through the **forest**.

forget When you forget something, you do not remember it.

Bert is going to the store. What did he **forget**? He **forgot** his pants.

fork A fork is a tool used to pick things up. Some forks are used to pick up food.

Waiter! This **fork** is dirty.

Bring me a clean **fork**, please.

Here is your clean **fork**, sir.

forward Forward means toward the front or the direction in which your feet are pointing.

The Monster Marching Band is marching **forward**.

four   Four is a number. Four is one more than three.

1...2...3...4...**four** bats! Wonderful!

fourteen   Fourteen is a number. Fourteen is ten plus four more.

Bert has ten small paper clips and four large paper clips. He has **fourteen** paper clips all together.

fox   A fox is a wild animal with a bushy tail.

The quick brown **fox** jumped over the lazy dog.

free   When something is free, it does not cost any money.

Nobody wants my pickle juice even though it is **free**. I don't understand it.

PICKLE JUICE

FREE!

free   When you are free, you can move in any direction.

Help! I can't move.

Ho-boy! It is good to be **free** again.

freeze   When something freezes, it turns to ice.

I had to wait for the pond to **freeze**. Now it is **frozen** and I can ice skate.

friend   A friend is someone you like who likes you.

Mr. Snuffle-upagus is my best **friend**.

frighten When you frighten someone, you make that person afraid.

Oscar likes to **frighten** Frazzle.

frog A frog is an animal that lives in or near water. It has webbed feet and strong back legs for jumping. A baby frog is a tadpole.

I can't believe my famous uncle, Kermit the **Frog**, was ever a tadpole.

To Robin, Fondly, Kermit

from From means out of.

Cookie Monster got some cookies **from** the cookie jar.

from From also means beginning with.

I know my letters **from** A to Z.

ABCDEFG
HIJKLMN
OPQRSTU
VWXYZ

front The front of something is the part that usually faces forward.

Grover's airplane has a propeller in **front**.

frown When you frown, you look unhappy or angry.

I look so handsome when I **frown**.

fruit A fruit is something that grows on a plant or a tree and holds seeds. Many fruits are sweet and good to eat.

One of these things does not belong in this **fruit** bowl.

An apple, a banana, and an orange are all **fruits**. That blue, furry thing is not a **fruit**.

Cookie Monster, get your paw out of the **fruit** bowl.

fuel Fuel is something that burns to make heat or energy. Wood, coal, gas, and oil are kinds of fuel.

The fire needs more **fuel.** I, Grover, am bringing another piece of wood.

full When something is full, it holds all that it can hold.

Here is a glass of ice-cold Figgy Fizz for my old buddy Bert.

But, Ernie, this glass is almost empty. I want a **full** glass.

Here is a **full** glass, Bert.

But this glass is **full** of marbles. I can't drink marbles.

fun When something is fun, you enjoy it.

You can have a lot of **fun** with marbles.

funny When something is funny, it makes you laugh.

How do you like my Halloween costume, Ernie?

Very **funny,** Bert.

fur Fur is soft, thick hair.

Some animals are covered with **fur.**

Herry Monster's **fur** is blue.

furniture Some of the movable things in a room are called furniture. Tables, chairs, and beds are pieces of furniture.

Hey, Herry, I'm not a piece of **furniture.**

Herry Monster is moving the **furniture.**

Of all the F words, my favorite is frown. That's a fact.

Can you say these terrible tongue twisters five times faster and faster?

Five fire-fighting flies.

Four frowning frogs.

A falling fairy falls faster than a fat flying fish flies.

A farmer found a famous feather.

game   A game is something that you play in a special way.

Hi, folks! This is Guy Smiley, everybody's favorite **game** show host, bringing you everybody's favorite **game**—HIDE AND SEEK!

Four friends from Sesame Street are hiding. If you want to play this **game,** you must find them.

HiDE and SEEK!

---

garage   A garage is a special place used to park cars.

The Count is driving his bat car into the **garage.**

garage   A garage is also a building where mechanics repair cars.

WE GUARANTEE OUR WORK!

The DAWN-to-DUSK GARAGE EXPERT BODYWORK!

OFFICE

REST ROOMS

GET KEY IN OFFICE

Prairie Dawn is a **garage** mechanic.
She works at the Dawn-to-Dusk **Garage.**

garbage   Garbage is leftover food that is thrown away.

The **garbage** collector is collecting the **garbage.** He empties the **garbage** cans into the **garbage** truck.

Beat it, buddy! This can is my home.

garden   A garden is a place where someone has planted flowers or vegetables.

Farmer Grover planted six different kinds of vegetables in his **garden.**

gate   A gate is a door in a fence or wall.

Herry Monster is opening the **gate.**

get   When you get something, you receive it.

Oscar **gets** his mud from the Mudman.

giant   Giant means very big.

Big Bird found a **giant** toothbrush. It belongs to Snuffle-upagus.

gift   A gift is a present.

Here, Mr. Snuffle-upagus, I made a **gift** for you.

Gee, thanks, Bird. Socks are just what I need.

Guess who gets these great gifts?

Can you match the gift with the Muppet?

giraffe A giraffe is the tallest animal in the world. It has a very long neck and eats leaves.

Is it true that a **giraffe** is the tallest animal in the world?

That's a fact.

give When you give something to someone, you hand it to that person.

Grover bought some flowers to **give** to his mother.

Thank you, Grover. These are the most beautiful flowers you ever **gave** me.

glad When you are glad, you are happy.

I'm **glad** you're my friend, Bird.

girl A girl is a child who will grow up to be a woman.

I am a **girl**.

My mother is a woman.

When I grow up, I will be a woman, too.

glass Glass is hard and smooth and breakable. You can see through most glass.

Three of these things belong together. One of these things is not the same.

A **glass** is something to drink from that is made out of **glass**.

A mirror, a window, and a **glass** slipper are all made out of **glass**. A cowgirl boot is made out of leather. The boot does not belong.

glasses   Glasses help people who do not see well to see better.

Mr. Chatterly wears **glasses** to help him see.

glove   A glove is a cover for your hand. It helps protect your hand and keeps it warm. Most gloves have places for five fingers.

Cookie the baker wears rubber **gloves** when he washes the dishes.

glue   Glue is wet and sticky and is used to join things together.

Ernie is using **glue** to put his model airplane together.

go   When you go, you move from one place to another.

Here I **go**! Good-by, everybod-ee!

Where did he **go**?

He **went** that way.

Now he is **gone**.

goat   A goat is an animal with hoofs and horns.

Farmer Grover's **goats** are in the vegetable garden.

I am a baby **goat**. I am a kid.

I am the kid's mother. I am a nanny **goat**.

I am the kid's father. I am a billy **goat**.

gold   Gold is a heavy yellow metal. Coins and jewelry are often made of gold.

At last I have found the buried treasure! Now I can count it. One piece of **gold**, two pieces of **gold**, three pieces of **gold** ...

gone When something is gone, it is no longer there.

Zounds! The cookies are **gone**!

The plate is **gone**!

Even the table is **gone**!

good Something that is good is done well.

That is a **good** trick, Betty Lou.

good When you are happy or healthy, you feel good.

Betty Lou has lots of energy. She feels **good.**

good A good person is kind and thinks of other people.

Would you like to share my sandwich, Sully?

Biff is a **good** friend.

goose A goose is a large bird. Some geese live on farms. Some geese are wild.

I am a baby **goose.** I am a gosling.

I am the gosling's mother. I am a **goose.**

I am the gosling's father. I am a gander.

The **geese** are swimming in the lake.

grab When you grab something, you take hold of it suddenly.

Grover, **grab** your balloon before it flies away.

grain A grain is a tiny piece of something.

When I am at the beach, I can count each **grain** of sand.

grain Grain is also the food that cereal and flour are made from.

I've just started a **grain** collection and I already have six different kinds of **grain**.

RICE BARLEY WHEAT OATS CORN RYE

grandparents Your grandparents are the parents of your father or mother.

GRANDFATHER MOTHER FATHER GRANDMOTHER
GRANDMOTHER GRANDFATHER

grape A grape is a small, round fruit that grows in bunches on vines.

Betty Lou is picking **grapes.**

grass Grass is a plant that covers the ground. Some grass is short and green. Some is tall and golden.

Farmer Grover's cows are eating the **grass** in the pasture.

great When something is great, it is bigger or better than usual.

Gee, Rodeo Rosie, that's a **great** trick!

grocery store A grocery store is a place where you can buy food and supplies which are called groceries. The person who sells groceries is the grocer.

Bert is buying **groceries** from the **grocer** at the **grocery store.**

grouch A grouch is someone who complains a lot.

What is **grouchier** than a **grouch**?

Two **grouches**!

ground The ground is the solid top part of the earth.

Grover's airplane is on the **ground.**

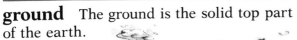

group A group is a collection of people or things.

A **group** of monsters is walking down the street.

grow When something grows, it becomes bigger.

Jack's beanstalk began to **grow,** and it kept on **growing** and **growing** and **growing.**

grow When you grow something, you put a seed or a plant in dirt and take care of it so that it will get bigger.

I like to **grow** many different kinds of plants in my backyard.

guard   A guard is someone who protects people or things.

The crossing **guard** helps the children to cross the street.

The life**guard** is **guarding** the swimmers.

guess   When you guess, you think of an answer without knowing for sure.

guest   A guest is someone who comes to visit.

Guess who will not be a **guest** for dinner again?

guitar   A guitar is a musical instrument with strings.

Cowboy Ernie is strumming his **guitar.**

? ?

Where are all the great words that begin with G—words like grimy, grubby, and grumpy?

A grouch guessing game

Can you find the garbage that begins with the letter **G**?